CONTENTS

KNOCK, KNOCK.

Who's there?

Jester.

Jester who?

Jester minute, isn't this the best joke book ever?!?!

Prepare yourself for laughs galore as you share these jokes with your friends and family. Keep a few up your comedy sleeve, and you'll always be able to make people chuckle, giggle, and groan as they join in the fun.

People will be knocking at your door just to hear the next hilarious encounter!

CHAPTER 1

Jokes to tell your friends

KNOCK, KNOCK.
Who's there?
Anya.
Anya who?
Anya marks, get set, go!

KNOCK, KNOCK.
Who's there?
Alf.
Alf who?
Alf feed your hamster while you're away!

KNOCK, KNOCK.
Who's there?
Alison.
Alison who?
Alison at the door to hear when you are coming!

6

KNOCK, KNOCK.
Who's there?
Adam.
Adam who?
Adamessy accident, can I come in?

KNOCK, KNOCK.
Who's there?
Wendy.
Wendy who?
Wendy want me to bring that DVD to you?

KNOCK, KNOCK.
Who's there?
Barbara.
Barbara who?
Barbara black sheep, have you any wool?

KNOCK, KNOCK.
Who's there?
Maya.
Maya who?
Maya come in for a while? My dad's not home yet.

KNOCK, KNOCK.
Who's there?
Danelle.
Danelle who?
Danelle pick you up from school tomorrow.

KNOCK, KNOCK.
Who's there?
Jacqueline.
Jacqueline who?
Jacqueline Hyde, watch out!

KNOCK, KNOCK.

Who's there?

David.

David who?

David my garden gnomes again, it's not funny.

KNOCK, KNOCK.

Who's there?

Belle.

Belle who?

Belle didn't work, so I had to knock.

KNOCK, KNOCK.

Who's there?

Paul.

Paul who?

Paul little lady has no one to visit her.

9

KNOCK, KNOCK.

Who's there?

Jennifer.

Jennifer who?

Jennifer-got I was coming, so I'm stuck outside!

KNOCK, KNOCK.

Who's there?

Iona.

Iona who?

Iona pony, Do you want a ride?

KNOCK, KNOCK.

Who's there?

Les.

Les who?

Les-agne, yummy!

KNOCK, KNOCK.
Who's there?
Arthur.
Arthur who?
Arthur any cookies left? I'm hungry!

KNOCK, KNOCK.
Who's there?
Ally.
Ally who?
Allygators aren't the same as crocodiles, you know!

KNOCK, KNOCK.
Who's there?
Doris.
Doris who?
Doris stuck, I can't move it an inch.

11

KNOCK, KNOCK.

Who's there?

Boo!

Boo who?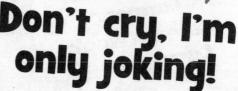

Don't cry, I'm only joking!

KNOCK, KNOCK.

Who's there?

Sonia.

Sonia who?

Sonia dress, you must have sat in it at the park.

KNOCK, KNOCK.

Who's there?
Juliet.
Juliet who?
Juliet a banana and now there's no fruit left.

KNOCK, KNOCK.
Who's there?
Carmen.
Carmen who?
Carmen play ball outside!

KNOCK, KNOCK.
Who's there?
Chris.
Chris who?
Chris-py bacon for breakfast, mmmm!

KNOCK, KNOCK.
Who's there?
Lionel.
Lionel who?
Lionel roar if you make it angry.

13

KNOCK, KNOCK.
Who's there?
Sandy.
Sandy who?
Sandy to know you're just next door if I need you!

KNOCK, KNOCK.
Who's there?
Dan.
Dan who?
Dan Dan DA! It's me! Surprise!

KNOCK, KNOCK.
Who's there?

Donna.
Donna who?

Donna you wanna come for pizza with us?

KNOCK, KNOCK.
Who's there?
Annie.
Annie who?
Annie where you want to go today?

KNOCK, KNOCK.
Who's there?
Tank.
Tank who?
Tank who very much!

KNOCK, KNOCK.
Who's there?
Phil.
Phil who?
Phil my bottle, would you? Our water is turned off.

KNOCK, KNOCK.
Who's there?
Stephie.
Stephie who?
Stephie nose and sore throat. I've caught a cold!

KNOCK, KNOCK.
Who's there?
Kay.
Kay who?
Kay sera, sera!

KNOCK, KNOCK.
Who's there?
Rose.
Rose who?
Rose at the crack of dawn to get here!

KNOCK, KNOCK.

Who's there?

Bernadette.

Bernadette who?

Bernadette my cupcake, can I have another one?

KNOCK, KNOCK.

Who's there?

Ivan.

Ivan who?

Ivan to go ice skating, will you come?

KNOCK, KNOCK.

Who's there?

Al.

Al who?

Al huff, and al puff, and al blow your house down!

KNOCK, KNOCK.
Who's there?
Ash.
Ash who?
Ooh, bless you!

KNOCK, KNOCK.
Who's there?
Althea.
Althea who?
Althea at the playground in half an hour.

KNOCK, KNOCK.
Who's there?
Eugenie.
Eugenie who?
Eugenie, grant my wishes!

KNOCK, KNOCK.

Who's there?

Halle.

Halle who?

Hallelujah! I thought you weren't going to answer.

KNOCK, KNOCK.

Who's there?

Lydia.

Lydia who?

Lydia recycling bin has blown across the road.

KNOCK, KNOCK.

Who's there?

Hugh.

Hugh who?

Hugh did you expect it to be?

KNOCK, KNOCK.

Who's there?

Norma Lee.

Norma Lee who?

Norma Lee I'd ring, but the doorbell's broken.

KNOCK, KNOCK.

Who's there?

Malik.

Malik who?

Malikkle sister loves her teddy bear!

KNOCK, KNOCK.

Who's there?

Joe.

Joe who?

Joe know where I can buy a newspaper?

CHAPTER 2
Jokes that'll split your sides

KNOCK, KNOCK.

Who's there?

Butter.

Butter who?

Butter grab your coat, it's cold! today.

KNOCK, KNOCK.

Who's there?

Ford.

Ford who?

Ford you'd like some company, so I've brought a movie!

KNOCK, KNOCK.

Who's there?

Theo.

Theo who?

Theo-ld lady next door needs someone to do her shopping!

KNOCK, KNOCK.
Who's there?
Ina.
Ina who?
Ina while, crocodile!

KNOCK, KNOCK.
Who's there?
Mama.
Mama who?
Mama mia, you ate all the pizza!

KNOCK, KNOCK.
Who's there?
Thea.
Thea who?
Thea later, alligator!

KNOCK, KNOCK.

Who's there?

Snowman.

Snowman who?

Snowman on earth can compare with my Dad. He's amazing!

KNOCK, KNOCK.

Who's there?

Sasha.

Sasha who?

Sasha noise coming from your party!

KNOCK, KNOCK.

Who's there?

Hans.

Hans who?

Hans up! Who's good at running?

KNOCK, KNOCK.
Who's there?
Anita.
Anita who?
Anita use your phone, please!

KNOCK, KNOCK.
Who's there?
Dwayne.
Dwayne who?
Dwaynes are blocked and smell really bad!

KNOCK, KNOCK.
Who's there?
Bella.
Bella who?
Bella the ball in my new dress!

KNOCK, KNOCK.
Who's there?
Otto.
Otto who?
Otto-matically assumed you'd be in today!

KNOCK, KNOCK.
Who's there?
Radio.
Radio who?
Radio-not, here I come!

KNOCK, KNOCK.
Who's there?
Alfred.
Alfred who?
Alfred of the dark, walk home with me!

KNOCK, KNOCK.

Who's there?

Leif.

Leif who?

Leif me alone, I'm in a bad mood!

KNOCK, KNOCK.

Who's there?

Emma.

Emma who?

Emma going into town, you-a coming?

KNOCK, KNOCK.

Who's there?

Sally.

Sally who?

Sally-brate, it's my birthday!

KNOCK, KNOCK.
Who's there?
Sid.
Sid who?
Sid you'd be ready, but you're not even dressed!

KNOCK, KNOCK.
Who's there?
Kenya.
Kenya who?
Kenya open the door please? I'm freezing!

KNOCK, KNOCK.
Who's there?
Archie.
Archie who?
Do you need a tissue?

KNOCK, KNOCK. Who's there? **Tom Sawyer.** Tom Sawyer who? **Tom Sawyer password when you were on the computer.**

KNOCK, KNOCK. Who's there? **Alison.** Alison who? **Alison Wonderland is the best book ever!**

KNOCK, KNOCK. Who's there? **Mia.** Mia who? **Meerkats are my top animal!**

KNOCK, KNOCK.
Who's there?
Eve.
Eve who?
Eve-n if you say sorry, I'm still cross!

KNOCK, KNOCK.
Who's there?
Wanda.
Wanda who?
Wanda come to mine for a sleepover?

KNOCK, KNOCK.
Who's there?
Ioni.
Ioni who?
Ioni small, I can't reach the doorbell!

KNOCK, KNOCK.

Who's there?

Abby.

Abby who?

Abby birthday!

KNOCK, KNOCK.

Who's there?

Karl.

Karl who?

Karl you on the phone, but you don't answer!

KNOCK, KNOCK.

Who's there?

Tess.

Tess who?

Tess who for your runny nose!

31

KNOCK, KNOCK.
Who's there?
Lettuce.
Lettuce who?
Lettuce in, I'm freezing!

KNOCK, KNOCK.
Who's there?
Ellie.
Ellie who?
Ellie-phants are my fave animal, what's yours?

KNOCK, KNOCK.
Who's there?
Kanga.
Kanga who?
No, kanga-roo, you dummy!

KNOCK, KNOCK.

Who's there?

Theodore.

Theodore who?

Theodore is stuck. Push it from your side!

KNOCK, KNOCK.

Who's there?

Luke.

Luke who?

Luke through the window, and you'll see!

KNOCK, KNOCK.

Who's there?

Dot.

Dot who?

Dot any tissues? By dose is running.

KNOCK, KNOCK.
Who's there?
Carla.
Carla who?
Carla taxi, I need to go!

KNOCK, KNOCK.
Who's there?
Wayne.
Wayne who?
Wayne drops keep falling on my head!

KNOCK, KNOCK.
Who's there?
Little old lady.
Little old lady who?
I didn't know you could yodel!

KNOCK, KNOCK.
Who's there?
Ronnie.
Ronnie who?
Ronnie away with me, I want to marry you!

KNOCK, KNOCK.
Who's there?
Frank Lee.
Frank Lee who?
Frank Lee, I think we've been snoozing on the job.

KNOCK, KNOCK.
Who's there?
Arianna.
Arianna who?
Arianna bunch of his friends are going to the park. You coming?

KNOCK, KNOCK.
Who's there?
Barbie.
Barbie who?
Barbie-cue at my place tonight. You're all invited!

KNOCK, KNOCK.
Who's there?
Eileen.
Eileen who?
Eileen over your fence when I need to get my ball back.

KNOCK, KNOCK.
Who's there?
Alvin.
Alvin who?
Alvin a great time!

CHAPTER 2
Jokes that'll cheer you up

KNOCK, KNOCK.
Who's there?
Dan.
Dan who?
Dan you oped de door? By dose is stuck!

KNOCK, KNOCK.
Who's there?
Pat.
Pat who?
Pat me on the back, I passed my big test!

KNOCK, KNOCK.
Who's there?
Matt.
Matt who?
Matthew, not Matt who, stupid!

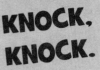

KNOCK, KNOCK.
Who's there?
Oink, oink.
Oink, oink who?
Make up your mind, are you a pig or an owl?

KNOCK, KNOCK.
Who's there?
Rupert.
Rupert who?
Rupert itching powder in my shirt?

KNOCK, KNOCK.
Who's there?
Tyler.
Tyler who?
Tyler for the kitchen wall, can I come in?

KNOCK, KNOCK.
Who's there?
Owl.
Owl who?
Owl aboard! Ready to set sail!

KNOCK, KNOCK.
Who's there?
Noah.
Noah who?
Noah don't know you at all, sorry!

KNOCK, KNOCK.
Who's there?
Jack.
Jack who?
Jack up the car, so I can fix the wheel!

KNOCK, KNOCK.
Who's there?
Juno.
Juno who?
Juno anywhere I can charge my phone?

KNOCK, KNOCK.
Who's there?
Lee King.
Lee King who?
Lee King water pipe out here, have you called a plumber?

KNOCK. KNOCK.
Who's there?
Alvin.
Alvin who?
Alvin you over with flowers and chocolates.

KNOCK, KNOCK.
Who's there?
Bud.
Bud who?
Bud why won't you lend me some cash?

KNOCK, KNOCK.
Who's there?
Andrew.
Andrew who?
Andrew on the wallpaper, and now she's in trouble.

KNOCK, KNOCK.
Who's there?
Rhoda.
Rhoda who?
Rhoda long way just to see you!

KNOCK, KNOCK.
Who's there?
Rhino.
Rhino who?
Rhino who you were out with last night!

KNOCK, KNOCK.
Who's there?
Michael.
Michael who?
Michael wash your car and make it sparkling clean!

KNOCK, KNOCK.
Who's there?
Ewan.
Ewan who?
Ewan-der if there's any point to all this, sometimes.

KNOCK, KNOCK.
Who's there?
Cam.
Cam who?
Cam out and we can play ball in the street.

KNOCK, KNOCK.
Who's there?
Logan.
Logan who?
Logan behold, it's a miracle!

KNOCK, KNOCK.
Who's there?
Noah.
Noah who?
Noah need to wipe your feet. come in!

KNOCK, KNOCK.
Who's there?
Lauren.
Lauren who?
Lauren order is very important these days.

KNOCK, KNOCK.
Who's there?
Alf.
Alf who?
Alf-ollow you wherever you go!

KNOCK, KNOCK.
Who's there?

Luke.
Luke who?

Luke how nice the weather is. You should come out!

45

KNOCK, KNOCK.
Who's there?
Alyssa.
Alyssa who?
Alyssa person would slam the door, but you're better than that.

KNOCK, KNOCK.
Who's there?
Lottie.
Lottie who?
Lottie use it will do me standing here if you won't open the door!

KNOCK, KNOCK.
Who's there?
Ivan.
Ivan who?
Ivan earache from standing in the snow for so long!

KNOCK, KNOCK.
Who's there?
Genie.
Genie who?
Genie-ed anything? Your wish is my command!

KNOCK, KNOCK.
Who's there?
Sherry.
Sherry who?
Sherry go to the dance tonight?

KNOCK, KNOCK.
Who's there?
Alfreda.
Alfreda who?
Alfreda you don't remember me after so long!

KNOCK, KNOCK.
Who's there?
Sidney.
Sidney who?
Sid needs your help to fix his car.

KNOCK, KNOCK.
Who's there?
Tristan.
Tristan who?
Tristan-ice girl like you to help your little sister.

KNOCK, KNOCK.
Who's there?
Albert.
Albert who?
Albert you can't guess who it is?!

48

KNOCK, KNOCK.
Who's there?
Linda.
Linda who?
Linda hand, I've got loads of luggage to carry!

KNOCK, KNOCK.
Who's there?
Ben.
Ben who?
Ben wondering where you were last month?

KNOCK, KNOCK.
Who's there?
Turner.
Turner who?
Turner round very slowly, there's a zombie behind you!

49

KNOCK, KNOCK.
Who's there?
Matt.
Matt who?
Matters not who I am, who are YOU?

KNOCK, KNOCK.
Who's there?
Sam.
Sam who?
Sam might say I'm a nuisance, knocking on your door all the time.

KNOCK, KNOCK.
Who's there?
Chris.
Chris who?
Christmas is here, yay!

KNOCK, KNOCK.

Who's there?

Doughnut.

Doughnut who?

Doughnut open the door too wide, or the cat will escape.

KNOCK, KNOCK.

Who's there?

Wendy.

Wendy who?

Wendy taxi arrives, I'll say goodbye.

KNOCK, KNOCK.

Who's there?

Fred.

Fred who?

Fred there's no more room in the car. You'll have to walk!

KNOCK, KNOCK.
Who's there?
Cows.
Cows who?
No, cows moo, not who!

KNOCK, KNOCK.
Who's there?
Shoes.
Shoes who?
Shoes me for asking, but would you go out with me?

KNOCK, KNOCK.
Who's there?
Ahab.
Ahab who?
Ahab a blocked nose and a sore throat.

52

CHAPTER 4
Jokes to tell your family

KNOCK, KNOCK.
Who's there?
Bill.
Bill who?
Bill-ding's on fire, get the firefighters!

KNOCK, KNOCK.
Who's there?
Alexis.
Alexis who?
Alexis here with me, can he see your new bike?

KNOCK, KNOCK.
Who's there?

Bea.
Bea who?

Bea a darling, and let me borrow your book.

KNOCK, KNOCK.
Who's there?
Whoo-oo-oooooo-ooo.
Whoo-oo-oooooo-ooo who?
Yikes! A haunted house!

KNOCK, KNOCK.
Who's there?
Tessa.
Tessa who?
Tessa long time for you to answer when I call!

KNOCK, KNOCK.
Who's there?
Roseanne.
Roseanne who?
Roseanne my tiptoes to reach the door knocker!

Knock, knock.
Who's there?
Parson.
Parson who?
Parson by your house and thought I'd say hi!

KNOCK, KNOCK.
Who's there?
You.
You who?
You-who, is anybody home?!

KNOCK, KNOCK.
Who's there?
Hardy.
Hardy who?
Hardy anyone around in the summer!

KNOCK, KNOCK.

Who's there?

Jerome.

Jerome who?

Jerome at last, where have you been?

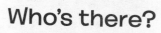

KNOCK, KNOCK.

Who's there?

Lacey.

Lacey who?

Lacey kids miss all the fun!

KNOCK, KNOCK.

Who's there?

Jackson.

Jackson who?

Jackson the road, I think he fell off his bike.

KNOCK, KNOCK.
Who's there?
Freddie.
Freddie who?
Freddie or not, here I come!

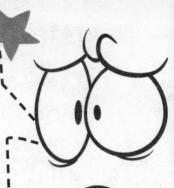

KNOCK, KNOCK.
Who's there?
Fred.
Fred who?
Fred I kicked my ball into your flowers, sorry!

KNOCK, KNOCK.
Who's there?
Iguana.
Iguana who?
Iguana hold your hand.

KNOCK, KNOCK.

Who's there?

Aila.

Aila who?

Aila-gs on a spider, I counted them!

KNOCK, KNOCK.

Who's there?

Courtney.

Courtney who?

Courtney glimpses of the people next door?

KNOCK, KNOCK.

Who's there?

Ivan.

Ivan who?

Ivan idea, let's play hide-and-seek!

KNOCK, KNOCK.
Who's there?
Lily.
Lily who?
Lily baby found her rattle!

KNOCK, KNOCK.
Who's there?
May.
May who?
May I borrow your phone, please?

KNOCK, KNOCK.
Who's there?
Theresa.
Theresa who?
Theresa green again, now that spring is here.

KNOCK, KNOCK.

Who's there?

Lucinda.

Lucinda who?

Lucinda sky with diamonds!

KNOCK, KNOCK.

Who's there?

Seymour.

Seymour who?

Seymour of the street if you open your curtains!

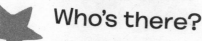

KNOCK, KNOCK.

Who's there?

Jess.

Jess who?

Jess wondering if you're allowed to go to the park?

61

KNOCK, KNOCK.

Who's there?

Fitz.

Fitz who?

Fitz not too much trouble, please can you give me a hand?

KNOCK, KNOCK.

Who's there?

Harriet.

Harriet who?

Harriet up, we're going to be late!

KNOCK, KNOCK.

Who's there?

Teddy.

Teddy who?

Teddy is Friday, so tomorrow it's the weekend!

KNOCK, KNOCK.
Who's there?

Grandma.
Grandma who?

Grandma-ning out here. Why don't you come out?

KNOCK, KNOCK.
Who's there?
Eden.
Eden who?
Eden my baby brother knows this is the right house.

KNOCK, KNOCK.
Who's there?
Maria.
Maria who?
Maria me please, I love you!

KNOCK, KNOCK.

Who's there?

Olive.

Olive who?

Olive the way you read to me, honey!

KNOCK, KNOCK.

Who's there?

Misty.

Misty who?

Misty delivery man, did he leave a box for me?

KNOCK, KNOCK.

Who's there?

Dexter.

Dexter who?

Dexter halls with boughs of holly!

KNOCK, KNOCK.
Who's there?
Arthur.
Arthur who?
Arthur the time, I think you're not listening to me!

KNOCK, KNOCK.
Who's there?
Mustafa.
Mustafa who?
Mustafa break soon, you've been working too hard!

KNOCK, KNOCK.
Who's there?
Constance.
Constance who?
Constance shouting next door is getting on my nerves!

KNOCK, KNOCK.

Who's there?

Police.

Police who?

Police fix your doorbell, my knuckles are getting sore!

KNOCK, KNOCK.

Who's there?

Bart.

Bart who?

Bart time you got up, it's 12 o'clock!

KNOCK, KNOCK.

Who's there?

Ida.

Ida who?

Ida know why no one will play outside!

KNOCK, KNOCK.

Who's there?

Jez.

Jez who?

Jez little old me!

KNOCK, KNOCK.

Who's there?

Walter.

Walter who?

Walter nice front door you have!

KNOCK, KNOCK.

Who's there?

Will.

Will who?

Will meet again, don't know where, don't know when ...

KNOCK, KNOCK.
Who's there?
Disaster.
Disaster who?
Disaster be my lucky day!

KNOCK, KNOCK.
Who's there?
Dana.
Dana who?
Dana go down the main road, it's flooded.

KNOCK, KNOCK.
Who's there?
Sarah.
Sarah who?
Sarah point to this joke?!

68

CHAPTER 5

Jokes that'll make you groan

KNOCK, KNOCK.
Who's there?
Barbara.
Barbara who?
Barbara for now, See you later!

KNOCK, KNOCK.
Who's there?
Brianna.
Brianna who?
Brianna cranberry baguette—do you want a bite?

KNOCK, KNOCK.
Who's there?
Anna.
Anna who?
Anna-nother one bites the dust.

KNOCK, KNOCK.

Who's there?

Edwin.

Edwin who?

Edwin every race if he ran a bit faster!

KNOCK, KNOCK.

Who's there?

Liz.

Liz who?

Liz go out to the football game.

KNOCK, KNOCK.

Who's there?

Ashley.

Ashley who?

Ashley, forget it, I'll go next door.

KNOCK, KNOCK.
Who's there?
Megan.
Megan who?
Megan her sister are moving across town.

KNOCK, KNOCK.
Who's there?
Allison.
Allison who?
Allison the TV tonight, he wins a prize!

KNOCK, KNOCK.
Who's there?
Otto.
Otto who?
Otto-graph hunting, are you famous?

KNOCK, KNOCK.
Who's there?
Cath.
Cath who?
Cath on delivery, pleathe?

KNOCK, KNOCK.
Who's there?
Crispin.
Crispin who?
Crispin fresh, that's how lettuce should be.

KNOCK, KNOCK.
Who's there?
Nat.
Nat who?
Nat a problem that we're here, is it?

74

KNOCK, KNOCK.

Who's there?

Acid.

Acid who?

Acid down and be quiet!

KNOCK, KNOCK.

Who's there?

Zizi.

Zizi who?

Zizi when you know how!

KNOCK, KNOCK.

Who's there?

Mason.

Mason who?

Mason john will be here on Saturday. Can he play with you?

75

KNOCK, KNOCK.
Who's there?
Avery.
Avery who?
Avery nice man just gave me lots of money!

KNOCK, KNOCK.
Who's there?
Maya.
Maya who?
Maya-nnaise is perfect with burgers. Do you have any?

KNOCK, KNOCK.
Who's there?
Austin.
Austin who?
Austink of garlic, I'm really sorry.

KNOCK, KNOCK.

Who's there?

Jez.

Jez who?

Jez amazing what you've done with this place!

KNOCK, KNOCK.

Who's there?

Lucas.

Lucas who?

Lucas a new game. Are you coming over?

KNOCK, KNOCK.

Who's there?

A big bear.

A big bear who?

A big bear bottom to make you laugh!

KNOCK, KNOCK.

Who's there?

Jethro.

Jethro who?

Jethro this ball at my window?

KNOCK, KNOCK.

Who's there?

Cecile.

Cecile who?

Ce-cile the w-windows, it's f-freezing outside!

KNOCK, KNOCK.

Who's there?

Annie.

Annie who?

Annie body want to come out to play?

KNOCK, KNOCK.

Who's there?

Dinah.

Dinah who?

Dinah-saurs are on the rampage! Look out!

KNOCK, KNOCK.

Who's there?

Irma.

Irma who?

Irma coming to see you. I've missed you so much!

KNOCK, KNOCK.

Who's there?

Lena.

Lena who?

Lena little closer, and I'll whisper it!

79

KNOCK, KNOCK.
Who's there?
Spider.
Spider who?
Spider what people say, I like you!

KNOCK, KNOCK.
Who's there?
Spell.
Spell who?
W-h-o. Easy!

KNOCK, KNOCK.
Who's there?
Hanson.
Hanson who?
Hanson my heart, I honestly didn't mean to kick the ball through your window.

KNOCK, KNOCK.
Who's there?
Samuel.
Samuel who?
Samuel have to move the bus, I can't get past it.

KNOCK, KNOCK.
Who's there?
Cyril.
Cyril who?
Cyril pleasure to see you!

KNOCK, KNOCK.
Who's there?
Owen.
Owen who?
Owen the saints, owen the saints, owen the saints come marching in ...

KNOCK, KNOCK.
Who's there?
Kent.
Kent who?
Kent you do your homework?

KNOCK, KNOCK.
Who's there?
Alec.
Alec who?
Alec-tricity has gone off. Let's light some candles!

KNOCK, KNOCK.
Who's there?
Vassar.
Vassar who?
Vassar matter, are you crying?

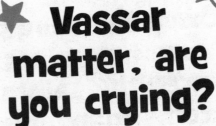

KNOCK, KNOCK.

Who's there?

Cass.

Cass who?

Cass more fish if you use live bait!

KNOCK, KNOCK.

Who's there?

Ivor.

Ivor who?

Ivor big bag of doughnuts to share if you let me in!

KNOCK, KNOCK.

Who's there?

Vassi.

Vassi who?

Vassi doing up there? He'll fall!

KNOCK, KNOCK.
Who's there?
Wanda.
Wanda who?
Wanda if there's anything good on TV tonight?

KNOCK, KNOCK.
Who's there?
Dina.
Dina who?
Dina hear me ring the bell?

KNOCK, KNOCK.
Who's there?
Carlo.
Carlo who?
Carload of people here to see you!

CHAPTER 6
Jokes to tell your teacher

KNOCK, KNOCK.
Who's there?
Celeste.
Celeste who?
Celeste time I'm coming over to help with your homework.

KNOCK, KNOCK.
Who's there?
Cath.
Cath who?
I knew you were nuts!

KNOCK, KNOCK.
Who's there?
Pizza!
Pizza who?
Pizza the action!

KNOCK, KNOCK.
Who's there?

Courtney.
Courtney who?

Courtney door, I can't get away!

KNOCK, KNOCK.
Who's there?
Matt.
Matt who?
Matt as well let me in, I'll just keep shouting if you don't!

KNOCK, KNOCK.
Who's there?
Candy.
Candy who?
Candy person who broke my window please confess?

KNOCK, KNOCK.
Who's there?
Juan.
Juan who?
Juan to go see a play?

KNOCK, KNOCK.
Who's there?
Anita.
Anita who?
Anita flower bed would make your house look better.

KNOCK, KNOCK.
Who's there?
Wilma.
Wilma who?
Wilma friend come out to play now?

KNOCK, KNOCK.

Who's there?

Izzy.

Izzy who?

Izzy allowed to come out to play, Mrs. Robson?

KNOCK, KNOCK.

Who's there?

Leona.

Leona who?

Leona of that car has parked in your spot!

KNOCK, KNOCK.

Who's there?

Toby.

Toby who?

Toby or not toby, that is the question!

KNOCK, KNOCK.
Who's there?
Ivana.
Ivana who?
Ivana use the bathroom, would you mind?

KNOCK, KNOCK.
Who's there?
Russell.
Russell who?
Russell be here soon. Everybody hide!

KNOCK, KNOCK.
Who's there?
Jilly.
Jilly who?
Jilly out here. Get my coat, please!

KNOCK, KNOCK.

Who's there?

Howl!

Howl who?

Howl you know if you don't open the door?

KNOCK, KNOCK.

Who's there?

Cher.

Cher who?

Cher your cake, or I'll tell everyone you're a meanie.

KNOCK, KNOCK.

Who's there?

Esau.

Esau who?

Esau a bus and ran to catch it.

KNOCK, KNOCK.

Who's there?

Barry.

Barry who?

Barry a bone by the house for your dog to find.

KNOCK, KNOCK.

Who's there?

Farmer.

Farmer who?

Farmer distance, I thought you were your brother!

KNOCK, KNOCK.

Who's there?

Brad.

Brad who?

Brad news, I'm afraid: you have to do your homework!

KNOCK, KNOCK.
Who's there?
Ben Hur.
Ben Hur who?
Ben Hur an hour. Didn't you hear me knocking?

KNOCK, KNOCK.
Who's there?
Jim.
Jim who?
Jim mind if I have a bite?

KNOCK, KNOCK.
Who's there?
Arnie.
Arnie who?
Arnie going to invite me in out of the rain?

KNOCK, KNOCK.

Who's there?

Phyllis.

Phyllis who?

Phyllis glass with water please, I'm thirsty!

KNOCK, KNOCK.

Who's there?

A little girl.

A little girl who?

A little girl who can't reach the doorbell!

KNOCK, KNOCK.

Who's there?

Thomas.

Thomas who?

Thomas just got a new kitten. Come and see it!

KNOCK, KNOCK.

Who's there?

Hayden.

Hayden who?

Hayden in your attic— try and find me!

KNOCK, KNOCK.

Who's there?

Adam.

Adam who?

Adam up, and tell me how much I owe you.

KNOCK, KNOCK.

Who's there?

Ginger.

Ginger who?

Ginger hear me singing in the shower?

KNOCK, KNOCK.
Who's there?
Marianne.
Marianne who?
Marianne instead of Grace if you love her!

KNOCK, KNOCK.
Who's there?
Emmett.
Emmett who?
Emmett your service!

KNOCK, KNOCK.
Who's there?
Señor.
Señor who?
Señor car was outside, so thought I'd say hi!

KNOCK, KNOCK.
Who's there?
McKee.
McKee who?
McKee won't turn in the lock!

KNOCK, KNOCK.
Who's there?
Sean.
Sean who?
Sean your hair again, have you?

KNOCK, KNOCK.
Who's there?
Esther.
Esther who?
Esther anything you want me to get for you in town?

KNOCK, KNOCK.

Who's there?

Amal.

Amal who?

Amal shook up, uh huh huh.

KNOCK, KNOCK.

Who's there?

Osborn.

Osborn who?

Osborn ten years ago today!

KNOCK, KNOCK.

Who's there?

Albie.

Albie who?

Albie a lot happier when you let me in!

KNOCK, KNOCK.
Who's there?
Sam.
Sam who?
Sam person as always knocks for you in the morning!

KNOCK, KNOCK.
Who's there?
Amit.
Amit who?
Amit your dad on his way to work!

KNOCK, KNOCK.
Who's there?
Eddie.
Eddie who?
Eddie-body there?

CHAPTER 7
Jokes that'll have you in stitches

KNOCK, KNOCK.

Who's there?

Eamonn.

Eamonn who?

Eamonn my way to the library, do you want a book?

KNOCK, KNOCK.

Who's there?

Rhoda.

Rhoda who?

Rhoda skateboard all the way here!

KNOCK, KNOCK.

Who's there?

Yvette.

Yvette who?

Yvette has given my cat some medicine.

KNOCK, KNOCK.

Who's there?

Chas.

Chas who?

Chas let me in, it's freezing out here!

KNOCK, KNOCK.

Who's there?

Sam.

Sam who?

Samtimes I wish you'd tell me what you're thinking.

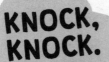

KNOCK, KNOCK.

Who's there?

Peggy.

Peggy who?

Peggy pardon, wrong house!

KNOCK, KNOCK.
Who's there?
Hailey.
Hailey who?
Hailey-n invader come to take over your planet!

KNOCK, KNOCK.
Who's there?
Elias.
Elias who?
Elias all the time, I never know whether to believe him.

KNOCK, KNOCK.
Who's there?
Don Giovanni.
Don giovanni who?
Don Giovanni come out shopping today?

KNOCK, KNOCK.

Who's there?

Ken.

Ken who?

Ken you move your bike, it's blocking the path!

KNOCK, KNOCK.

Who's there?

Scott.

Scott who?

Scott to be said, your bedroom is a mess!

KNOCK, KNOCK.

Who's there?

Harry.

Harry who?

Harry up, we'll be late for gym!

KNOCK, KNOCK.
Who's there?
Water.
Water who?
Water you doing here?!

KNOCK, KNOCK.
Who's there?
Khan.
Khan who?
Khan you lend me some money, please?

KNOCK, KNOCK.
Who's there?
Tex.
Tex who?
Tex you ages to answer your door!

KNOCK, KNOCK.

Who's there?

Alpaca.

Alpaca who?

Alpaca my things and move in tomorrow!

KNOCK, KNOCK.

Who's there?

Alva.

Alva who?

Alva chocolate bar is better than none!

KNOCK, KNOCK.

Who's there?

Queen.

Queen who?

Queen your windows, they're filthy!

107

KNOCK, KNOCK.

Who's there?

Mabel.

Mabel who?

Mabel has broken, and now so has yours!

KNOCK, KNOCK.

Who's there?

Hugo.

Hugo who?

Hugo-ing to open this door, or what?

KNOCK, KNOCK.

Who's there?

Ezra.

Ezra who?

Ezra no way we can coax you to come to the party?

KNOCK, KNOCK.
Who's there?
Francis.
Francis who?
Francis a lovely country, have you visited?

KNOCK, KNOCK.
Who's there?
Isadore.
Isadore who?
Isadore to school locked? Yay!

KNOCK, KNOCK.
Who's there?

Trudi.
Trudi who?

Tru—di caterpillar does turn into a butterfly.

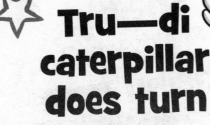

109

KNOCK, KNOCK.

Who's there?

Mary Lee.

Mary lee who?

Mary Lee, Mary Lee, life is but a dream. Row, row, row your boat ...

KNOCK, KNOCK.

Who's there?

May.

May who?

May the force be with you!

KNOCK, KNOCK.

Who's there?

Shelby.

Shelby who?

Shelby here in a minute, everybody hide!

KNOCK, KNOCK.
Who's there?
Abbott.
Abbott who?
Abbott time you got up! It's late!

KNOCK, KNOCK.
Who's there?
Polly.
Polly who?
Polly your hand out of that refrigerator—no snacking!

KNOCK, KNOCK.
Who's there?
Rufus.
Rufus who?
Rufus on fire, call the firefighters!

KNOCK, KNOCK.
Who's there?
Amanda.
Amanda who?
Amanda the car, and I think I'm stuck!

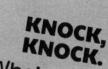

KNOCK, KNOCK.
Who's there?
Major.
Major who?
Major mind up yet?

KNOCK, KNOCK.
Who's there?
Ivor.
Ivor who?
Ivor go left or go right, but you have to choose!

113

KNOCK, KNOCK.

Who's there?

Ivan.

Ivan who?

Ivan enormous cake, big enough to share!

KNOCK, KNOCK.

Who's there?

Farrah.

Farrah who?

Farrah lot of people, Saturday is the best day of the week.

KNOCK, KNOCK.

Who's there?

Champ.

Champ who?

Shampoo? But I'm not washing my hair!

CHAPTER 8
Jokes to tell your dog

KNOCK, KNOCK.
Who's there?
Joan.
Joan who?
Joan call us, we'll call you!

KNOCK, KNOCK.
Who's there?
Irene.
Irene who?
Irene the bell, but you never answer.

KNOCK, KNOCK.
Who's there?
Holly.
Holly who?
Holly-lujah, the Christmas tree is decorated!

KNOCK, KNOCK.
Who's there?
Piet.
Piet who?
Piet of advice for you— don't eat yellow snow!

KNOCK, KNOCK.
Who's there?
Minerva.
Minerva who?
Minerva-s wreck, I can't take it another minute!

KNOCK, KNOCK.
Who's there?
Lion.
Lion who?
Lion in bed all day is just lazy!

117

Knock, knock.
Who's there?
Juan.
Juan who?
Juan to hear more jokes?

KNOCK, KNOCK.
Who's there?
Dozen.
Dozen who?
Dozen anyone ever read the newspapers?

KNOCK, KNOCK.
Who's there?
Dummy.
Dummy who?
Dummy a sandwich, will you? I'm hungry!

KNOCK, KNOCK.

Who's there?

Jess.

Jess who?

Jess wondering if you're coming out?

KNOCK, KNOCK.

Who's there?

Isaac.

Isaac who?

Isaactly how long are you going to talk?

KNOCK, KNOCK.

Who's there?

Earl.

Earl who?

Earl be glad to see you again!

KNOCK, KNOCK.

Who's there?

Dwight.

Dwight who?

Dwight thing to do is to let me in!

KNOCK, KNOCK.

Who's there?

Jimmy.

Jimmy who?

Jimmy a hug, you know you want to!

KNOCK, KNOCK.

Who's there?

Ammonia.

Ammonia who?

Ammonia little kid, give me a break!

KNOCK,
KNOCK.
Who's there?
Dishes.
Dishes who?
**Dishes such
a bad joke!**

KNOCK,
KNOCK.
Who's there?
Cynthia.
Cynthia who?
**Cynthia been
gone, I've
really missed
you!**

KNOCK,
KNOCK.
Who's there?
Beaver.
Beaver who?

Beaver-y quiet, and
we can sneak out!

KNOCK, KNOCK.

Who's there?

Khan.

Khan who?

Khan't go out, i'm grounded!

KNOCK, KNOCK.

Who's there?

Greta.

Greta who?

Greta coat, and come and play in the snow!

KNOCK, KNOCK.

Who's there?

Minnie.

Minnie who?

Minnie more jokes where this one came from!

KNOCK, KNOCK.
Who's there?
Giraffe.
Giraffe who?
Giraffe to stand there? You're in the way!

KNOCK, KNOCK.
Who's there?
Major.
Major who?
Major jump, ha ha!

KNOCK, KNOCK.
Who's there?
Paula.
Paula who?
Paula door open, and let the sun shine in!

123

KNOCK, KNOCK.
Who's there?
Colin.
Colin who?
Colin you on the phone all day!

KNOCK, KNOCK.
Who's there?
Daisy.
Daisy who?
Daisy know you're as pretty as a picture?

KNOCK, KNOCK.
Who's there?
Sacha.
Sacha who?
Sacha fuss over nothing!

KNOCK, KNOCK.

Who's there?

Josie.

Josie who?

Josie anyone else out here? It's me!

KNOCK, KNOCK.

Who's there?

Joaquin.

Joaquin who?

Joaquin down the street, looking for my cat ...

KNOCK, KNOCK.

Who's there?

Hairy monster.

Hairy monster who?

How many hairy monsters do you know?!

125

KNOCK, KNOCK.
Who's there?
Beryl.
Beryl who?
Beryl of laughs!

KNOCK, KNOCK.
Who's there?
Clara.
Clara who?
Clara space, and I'll bring in your new tv!

KNOCK, KNOCK.
Who's there?
Euan.
Euan who?
Euan to marry me? You've made me so happy!

KNOCK, KNOCK.

Who's there?

Frank.

Frank who?

Frank you for feeding my cat while I was away.

KNOCK, KNOCK.

Who's there?

Paris.

Paris who?

Paris the thought!

KNOCK, KNOCK.

Who's there?

Misha.

Misha who?

Misha loads when you're away!

KNOCK, KNOCK.
Who's there?
Ooze.
Ooze who?
Ooze been sitting in my swing?

KNOCK, KNOCK.
Who's there?
Carmen.
Carmen who?
Carmen go roller skating with me!

KNOCK, KNOCK.
Who's there?
Augusta.
Augusta who?
Augusta wind has blown my kite into your tree.